MW01226646

If found please return this

GO KARTING
LOG BOOK

to:

_____

_____

RACE EVENT		DATE
LOCATION		
KART NUMBER		/ /

RACE NUMBER IN ROW		CURRENT STANDING	
WEATHER CONDITION	☀ ☔ ❄ ⛈ 💨	TIME OF YEAR	🌷 ☀ 🍃 ❄
TIRES USED	⊛	RACE START	
		RACE FINISH	
ENGINE SIZE		FINISHING POSITION	🏁

TYRE PRESSURE

START POSITION

FRONT	REAR

LAPS COMPLETED

1ST ROUND AT

FASTEST TIME

FASTEST LAP

FURTHER OBSERVATIONS

RACE EVENT		DATE
LOCATION		
KART NUMBER		/ /

RACE NUMBER IN ROW		CURRENT STANDING	
WEATHER CONDITION	☀ ☔ ❄ ⛈ 🌬	TIME OF YEAR	🌷 ☀ 🍃 ❄
TIRES USED	◉	RACE START	🕐
		RACE FINISH	
ENGINE SIZE	🔧	FINISHING POSITION	🏁

TYRE PRESSURE		START POSITION
FRONT	REAR	
		LAPS COMPLETED
		1ST ROUND AT

FASTEST TIME	FASTEST LAP

FURTHER OBSERVATIONS

RACE EVENT		DATE
LOCATION		
KART NUMBER		/ /

RACE NUMBER IN ROW		CURRENT STANDING	
WEATHER CONDITION	☀ ☁ ❄ ⚡ 🌬	TIME OF YEAR	🌷 ☀ 🍁 ❄
TIRES USED	⊚	RACE START	🕐
		RACE FINISH	
ENGINE SIZE		FINISHING POSITION	🏁

TYRE PRESSURE		START POSITION
FRONT	REAR	
		LAPS COMPLETED
		1ST ROUND AT

FASTEST TIME	FASTEST LAP

FURTHER OBSERVATIONS

RACE EVENT		DATE
LOCATION		
KART NUMBER		/ /

RACE NUMBER IN ROW		CURRENT STANDING	
WEATHER CONDITION	☀ ☁ ❄ ⛈ 〰	TIME OF YEAR	🌷 ☀ 🍂 ❄
TIRES USED	⊕	RACE START	🕐
		RACE FINISH	
ENGINE SIZE	🔧	FINISHING POSITION	🏁

TYRE PRESSURE		START POSITION
FRONT	REAR	
		LAPS COMPLETED
		1ST ROUND AT

FASTEST TIME	FASTEST LAP

FURTHER OBSERVATIONS

RACE EVENT		DATE
LOCATION		
KART NUMBER		/ /

RACE NUMBER IN ROW		CURRENT STANDING	
WEATHER CONDITION	☀ ☁ ❄ ⛈ 💨	TIME OF YEAR	🌷 ☀ 🍁 ❄
TIRES USED	⚙	RACE START	🕐
		RACE FINISH	
ENGINE SIZE	🔧	FINISHING POSITION	🏁

TYRE PRESSURE		START POSITION
FRONT	REAR	
		LAPS COMPLETED
		1ST ROUND AT

FASTEST TIME	FASTEST LAP

FURTHER OBSERVATIONS

RACE EVENT		DATE
LOCATION		
KART NUMBER		/ /

RACE NUMBER IN ROW		CURRENT STANDING	
WEATHER CONDITION	☀ ☁ ❄ ⛈ 🌬	TIME OF YEAR	🌷 ☀ 🍂 ❄
TIRES USED	◉	RACE START	🕐
		RACE FINISH	
ENGINE SIZE	🔧	FINISHING POSITION	🏁

TYRE PRESSURE		START POSITION
FRONT	REAR	
		LAPS COMPLETED
		1ST ROUND AT

FASTEST TIME	FASTEST LAP

FURTHER OBSERVATIONS

RACE EVENT		DATE
LOCATION		
KART NUMBER		/ /

RACE NUMBER IN ROW		CURRENT STANDING	
WEATHER CONDITION	☀ ☁ ❄ ⚡ 〰	TIME OF YEAR	🌷 ☀ 🍂 ❄
TIRES USED	◉	RACE START	🕐
		RACE FINISH	
ENGINE SIZE	⚙	FINISHING POSITION	🏁

TYRE PRESSURE		START POSITION
FRONT	REAR	
		LAPS COMPLETED
		1ST ROUND AT

FASTEST TIME	FASTEST LAP

FURTHER OBSERVATIONS

RACE EVENT		DATE
LOCATION		
KART NUMBER		/ /

RACE NUMBER IN ROW		CURRENT STANDING	
WEATHER CONDITION	☀ ☁ ❄ ⛈ 🌬	TIME OF YEAR	🌷 ☀ 🍃 ❄
TIRES USED	⚙	RACE START	🕐
		RACE FINISH	
ENGINE SIZE	🔧	FINISHING POSITION	🏁

TYRE PRESSURE		START POSITION
FRONT	REAR	
		LAPS COMPLETED
		1ST ROUND AT

FASTEST TIME	FASTEST LAP

FURTHER OBSERVATIONS

RACE EVENT		DATE
LOCATION		
KART NUMBER		/ /

RACE NUMBER IN ROW		CURRENT STANDING	
WEATHER CONDITION	☀ ☁ ❄ ⛈ 🌬	TIME OF YEAR	🌷 ☀ 🍂 ❄
TIRES USED	◉	RACE START	⊕
		RACE FINISH	
ENGINE SIZE	⚙	FINISHING POSITION	🏁

TYRE PRESSURE		START POSITION
FRONT	REAR	
		LAPS COMPLETED
		1ST ROUND AT

FASTEST TIME	FASTEST LAP

FURTHER OBSERVATIONS

RACE EVENT		DATE
LOCATION		
KART NUMBER		/ /

RACE NUMBER IN ROW		CURRENT STANDING	
WEATHER CONDITION	☀ ☁ ❄ ⛈ 🌬	TIME OF YEAR	🌷 ☀ 🍂 ❄
TIRES USED	⊚	RACE START	🕐
		RACE FINISH	
ENGINE SIZE	⬗	FINISHING POSITION	🏁

TYRE PRESSURE		START POSITION
FRONT	**REAR**	
		LAPS COMPLETED
		1ST ROUND AT

FASTEST TIME	FASTEST LAP

FURTHER OBSERVATIONS

RACE EVENT		DATE
LOCATION		
KART NUMBER		/ /

RACE NUMBER IN ROW		CURRENT STANDING	
WEATHER CONDITION	☀ ☁ ❄ ⚡ 〜	TIME OF YEAR	🌷 ☀ 🍃 ❄
TIRES USED	⚙	RACE START	🕐
		RACE FINISH	
ENGINE SIZE	🔧	FINISHING POSITION	🏁

TYRE PRESSURE		START POSITION
FRONT	REAR	
		LAPS COMPLETED
		1ST ROUND AT

FASTEST TIME	FASTEST LAP

FURTHER OBSERVATIONS

RACE EVENT		DATE
LOCATION		
KART NUMBER		/ /

RACE NUMBER IN ROW		CURRENT STANDING	
WEATHER CONDITION	☀ ☁ ❄ ⛈ 🌬	TIME OF YEAR	🌷 ☀ 🍃 ❄
TIRES USED	⊛	RACE START	🕐
		RACE FINISH	
ENGINE SIZE		FINISHING POSITION	🏁

TYRE PRESSURE		START POSITION
FRONT	REAR	
		LAPS COMPLETED
		1ST ROUND AT

FASTEST TIME	FASTEST LAP

FURTHER OBSERVATIONS

RACE EVENT		DATE
LOCATION		
KART NUMBER		/ /

RACE NUMBER IN ROW		CURRENT STANDING	
WEATHER CONDITION	☀ ☁ ❄ ⚡ 💨	TIME OF YEAR	🌷 ☀ 🍂 ❄
TIRES USED	⚙	RACE START	🕐
		RACE FINISH	
ENGINE SIZE	🔧	FINISHING POSITION	🏁

TYRE PRESSURE		START POSITION
FRONT	REAR	
		LAPS COMPLETED
		1ST ROUND AT

FASTEST TIME	FASTEST LAP

FURTHER OBSERVATIONS

RACE EVENT		DATE
LOCATION		
KART NUMBER		/ /

RACE NUMBER IN ROW		CURRENT STANDING	
WEATHER CONDITION	☀ ☁ ❄ ⛈ 🌬	TIME OF YEAR	🌷 ☀ 🍃 ❄
TIRES USED	⊚	RACE START	🕐
		RACE FINISH	
ENGINE SIZE		FINISHING POSITION	🏁

TYRE PRESSURE		START POSITION
FRONT	REAR	
		LAPS COMPLETED
		1ST ROUND AT

FASTEST TIME	FASTEST LAP

FURTHER OBSERVATIONS

RACE EVENT		DATE
LOCATION		
KART NUMBER		/ /

RACE NUMBER IN ROW		CURRENT STANDING	
WEATHER CONDITION	☀ ☁ ❄ ⛈ 🌬	TIME OF YEAR	🌷 ☀ 🍁 ❄
TIRES USED	◉	RACE START	🕐
		RACE FINISH	
ENGINE SIZE	🔧	FINISHING POSITION	🏁

TYRE PRESSURE		START POSITION
FRONT	REAR	
		LAPS COMPLETED
		1ST ROUND AT

FASTEST TIME	FASTEST LAP

FURTHER OBSERVATIONS

RACE EVENT		DATE
LOCATION		
KART NUMBER		/ /

RACE NUMBER IN ROW		CURRENT STANDING	
WEATHER CONDITION	☀ ☁ ❄ ⛈ 🌬	TIME OF YEAR	🌷 ☀ 🍃 ❄
TIRES USED	⊕	RACE START	🕐
		RACE FINISH	
ENGINE SIZE		FINISHING POSITION	🏁

TYRE PRESSURE		START POSITION
FRONT	REAR	
		LAPS COMPLETED
		1ST ROUND AT

FASTEST TIME	FASTEST LAP

FURTHER OBSERVATIONS

RACE EVENT		DATE
LOCATION		
KART NUMBER		/ /

RACE NUMBER IN ROW		CURRENT STANDING	
WEATHER CONDITION	☀ ☁ ❄ ⚡ 〰	TIME OF YEAR	🌷 ☀ 🍂 ❄
TIRES USED	⊛	RACE START	🕐
		RACE FINISH	
ENGINE SIZE		FINISHING POSITION	🏁

TYRE PRESSURE

START POSITION

FRONT	REAR

LAPS COMPLETED

1ST ROUND AT

FASTEST TIME

FASTEST LAP

FURTHER OBSERVATIONS

RACE EVENT		DATE
LOCATION		
KART NUMBER		/ /

RACE NUMBER IN ROW		CURRENT STANDING	
WEATHER CONDITION	☀ ☁ ❄ ⛈ 🌬	TIME OF YEAR	🌷 ☀ 🍃 ❄
TIRES USED	⊚	RACE START	🕐
		RACE FINISH	
ENGINE SIZE	🔧	FINISHING POSITION	🏁

TYRE PRESSURE / START POSITION

FRONT	REAR

LAPS COMPLETED

1ST ROUND AT

FASTEST TIME / FASTEST LAP

FURTHER OBSERVATIONS

RACE EVENT		DATE
LOCATION		
KART NUMBER		/ /

RACE NUMBER IN ROW		CURRENT STANDING	
WEATHER CONDITION	☀ ☁ ❄ ⚡ 〜	TIME OF YEAR	🌷 ☀ 🍁 ❄
TIRES USED	◎	RACE START	🕐
		RACE FINISH	
ENGINE SIZE	⚙	FINISHING POSITION	🏁

TYRE PRESSURE		START POSITION
FRONT	REAR	
		LAPS COMPLETED
		1ST ROUND AT

FASTEST TIME	FASTEST LAP

FURTHER OBSERVATIONS

RACE EVENT		DATE
LOCATION		
KART NUMBER		/ /

RACE NUMBER IN ROW		CURRENT STANDING	
WEATHER CONDITION	☀ ☁ ❄ ⛈ 🌬	TIME OF YEAR	🌷 ☀ 🍃 ❄
TIRES USED	⚙	RACE START	🕐
		RACE FINISH	
ENGINE SIZE		FINISHING POSITION	🏁

TYRE PRESSURE		START POSITION
FRONT	REAR	
		LAPS COMPLETED
		1ST ROUND AT

FASTEST TIME	FASTEST LAP

FURTHER OBSERVATIONS

RACE EVENT		DATE
LOCATION		
KART NUMBER		/ /

RACE NUMBER IN ROW		CURRENT STANDING	
WEATHER CONDITION	☀ ☁ ❄ ⚡ 〰	TIME OF YEAR	🌷 ☀ 🍂 ❄
TIRES USED	◉	RACE START	🕐
		RACE FINISH	
ENGINE SIZE		FINISHING POSITION	🏁

TYRE PRESSURE		START POSITION
FRONT	REAR	
		LAPS COMPLETED
		1ST ROUND AT

FASTEST TIME	FASTEST LAP

FURTHER OBSERVATIONS

RACE EVENT		DATE
LOCATION		
KART NUMBER		/ /

RACE NUMBER IN ROW		CURRENT STANDING	
WEATHER CONDITION	☀ ☁ ❄ ⛈ ≋	TIME OF YEAR	🌷 ☀ 🍃 ❄
TIRES USED	◉	RACE START	🕐
		RACE FINISH	
ENGINE SIZE	⚙	FINISHING POSITION	🏁

TYRE PRESSURE		START POSITION
FRONT	REAR	
		LAPS COMPLETED
		1ST ROUND AT

FASTEST TIME	FASTEST LAP

FURTHER OBSERVATIONS

RACE EVENT		DATE
LOCATION		
KART NUMBER		/ /

RACE NUMBER IN ROW		CURRENT STANDING	
WEATHER CONDITION	☀ ☁ ❄ ⚡ 〰	TIME OF YEAR	🌷 ☀ 🍂 ❄
TIRES USED	⚙	RACE START	🕐
		RACE FINISH	
ENGINE SIZE	🔧	FINISHING POSITION	🏁

TYRE PRESSURE

START POSITION

FRONT	REAR

LAPS COMPLETED

1ST ROUND AT

FASTEST TIME	FASTEST LAP

FURTHER OBSERVATIONS

RACE EVENT		DATE
LOCATION		
KART NUMBER		/ /

RACE NUMBER IN ROW		CURRENT STANDING	
WEATHER CONDITION	☀ ☁ ❄ ⛈ 🌬	TIME OF YEAR	🌷 ☀ 🍃 ❄
TIRES USED	⚙	RACE START	🕐
		RACE FINISH	
ENGINE SIZE	⚙	FINISHING POSITION	🏁

TYRE PRESSURE		START POSITION
FRONT	REAR	
		LAPS COMPLETED
		1ST ROUND AT

FASTEST TIME	FASTEST LAP

FURTHER OBSERVATIONS

RACE EVENT		DATE
LOCATION		
KART NUMBER		/ /

RACE NUMBER IN ROW		CURRENT STANDING	
WEATHER CONDITION	☀ ☁ ❄ ⛈ 🌬	TIME OF YEAR	🌷 ☀ 🍃 ❄
TIRES USED	◎	RACE START	🕐
		RACE FINISH	
ENGINE SIZE		FINISHING POSITION	🏁

TYRE PRESSURE		START POSITION
FRONT	REAR	
		LAPS COMPLETED
		1ST ROUND AT

FASTEST TIME	FASTEST LAP

FURTHER OBSERVATIONS

RACE EVENT		DATE
LOCATION		
KART NUMBER		/ /

RACE NUMBER IN ROW		CURRENT STANDING	
WEATHER CONDITION	☀ ☁ ❄ ⛈ 🌬	TIME OF YEAR	🌷 ☀ 🍃 ❄
TIRES USED	⚙	RACE START	🕐
		RACE FINISH	
ENGINE SIZE	⚙	FINISHING POSITION	🏁

TYRE PRESSURE		START POSITION
FRONT	**REAR**	
		LAPS COMPLETED
		1ST ROUND AT

FASTEST TIME	FASTEST LAP

FURTHER OBSERVATIONS

RACE EVENT		DATE
LOCATION		
KART NUMBER		/ /

RACE NUMBER IN ROW		CURRENT STANDING	
WEATHER CONDITION	☀ ☁ ❄ ⛈ 🌬	TIME OF YEAR	🌷 ☀ 🍃 ❄
TIRES USED	◉	RACE START	🕐
		RACE FINISH	
ENGINE SIZE	🔧	FINISHING POSITION	🏁

TYRE PRESSURE		START POSITION
FRONT	REAR	
		LAPS COMPLETED
		1ST ROUND AT

FASTEST TIME	FASTEST LAP

FURTHER OBSERVATIONS

RACE EVENT		DATE
LOCATION		
KART NUMBER		/ /

RACE NUMBER IN ROW		CURRENT STANDING	
WEATHER CONDITION	☀ ☁ ❄ ⛈ 🌬	TIME OF YEAR	🌷 ☀ 🍃 ❄
TIRES USED	⚙	RACE START	🕐
		RACE FINISH	
ENGINE SIZE	🔧	FINISHING POSITION	🏁

TYRE PRESSURE		START POSITION
FRONT	REAR	
		LAPS COMPLETED
		1ST ROUND AT

FASTEST TIME	FASTEST LAP

FURTHER OBSERVATIONS

RACE EVENT		DATE
LOCATION		
KART NUMBER		/ /

RACE NUMBER IN ROW		CURRENT STANDING	
WEATHER CONDITION	☀ ☁ ❄ ⚡ 〰	TIME OF YEAR	🌷 ☀ 🍂 ❄
TIRES USED	◉	RACE START	🕐
		RACE FINISH	
ENGINE SIZE	🔧	FINISHING POSITION	🏁

TYRE PRESSURE		START POSITION
FRONT	REAR	
		LAPS COMPLETED
		1ST ROUND AT

FASTEST TIME	FASTEST LAP

FURTHER OBSERVATIONS

RACE EVENT		DATE
LOCATION		
KART NUMBER		/ /

RACE NUMBER IN ROW		CURRENT STANDING	
WEATHER CONDITION	☀ ☁ ❄ ⛈ 🌬	TIME OF YEAR	🌷 ☀ 🍃 ❄
TIRES USED	⊕	RACE START	🕐
		RACE FINISH	
ENGINE SIZE		FINISHING POSITION	🏁

TYRE PRESSURE		START POSITION
FRONT	REAR	
		LAPS COMPLETED
		1ST ROUND AT

FASTEST TIME	FASTEST LAP

FURTHER OBSERVATIONS

RACE EVENT		DATE
LOCATION		
KART NUMBER		/ /

RACE NUMBER IN ROW		CURRENT STANDING	
WEATHER CONDITION	☀ ☁ ❄ ⛈ 🌬	TIME OF YEAR	🌷 ☀ 🍃 ❄
TIRES USED	⬤	RACE START	🕐
		RACE FINISH	
ENGINE SIZE	🔧	FINISHING POSITION	🏁

TYRE PRESSURE		START POSITION
FRONT	REAR	
		LAPS COMPLETED
		1ST ROUND AT

FASTEST TIME	FASTEST LAP

FURTHER OBSERVATIONS

RACE EVENT		DATE
LOCATION		
KART NUMBER		/ /

RACE NUMBER IN ROW		CURRENT STANDING	
WEATHER CONDITION	☀ ☁ ❄ ⛈ 🌬	TIME OF YEAR	🌷 ☀ 🍃 ❄
TIRES USED	⚙	RACE START / RACE FINISH	🕐
ENGINE SIZE	🔧	FINISHING POSITION	🏁

TYRE PRESSURE

FRONT	REAR

START POSITION

LAPS COMPLETED

1ST ROUND AT

FASTEST TIME

FASTEST LAP

FURTHER OBSERVATIONS

RACE EVENT		DATE
LOCATION		
KART NUMBER		/ /

RACE NUMBER IN ROW		CURRENT STANDING	
WEATHER CONDITION	☀ ☁ ❄ ⛈ 🌬	TIME OF YEAR	🌷 ☀ 🍁 ❄
TIRES USED	⚙	RACE START	🕐
		RACE FINISH	
ENGINE SIZE		FINISHING POSITION	🏁

TYRE PRESSURE		START POSITION
FRONT	REAR	
		LAPS COMPLETED
		1ST ROUND AT

FASTEST TIME	FASTEST LAP

FURTHER OBSERVATIONS

RACE EVENT		DATE
LOCATION		
KART NUMBER		/ /

RACE NUMBER IN ROW		CURRENT STANDING	
WEATHER CONDITION	☀ ☁ ❄ ⛈ 🌬	TIME OF YEAR	🌷 ☀ 🍂 ❄
TIRES USED	⚙	RACE START	🕐
		RACE FINISH	
ENGINE SIZE	🔧	FINISHING POSITION	🏁

TYRE PRESSURE		START POSITION
FRONT	REAR	
		LAPS COMPLETED
		1ST ROUND AT

FASTEST TIME	FASTEST LAP

FURTHER OBSERVATIONS

RACE EVENT		DATE
LOCATION		
KART NUMBER		/ /

RACE NUMBER IN ROW		CURRENT STANDING	
WEATHER CONDITION	☀ ☁ ❄ ⛈ 🌬	TIME OF YEAR	🌷 ☀ 🍃 ❄
TIRES USED	⚙	RACE START	🕐
		RACE FINISH	
ENGINE SIZE	🔧	FINISHING POSITION	🏁

TYRE PRESSURE		START POSITION
FRONT	REAR	
		LAPS COMPLETED
		1ST ROUND AT

FASTEST TIME	FASTEST LAP

FURTHER OBSERVATIONS

RACE EVENT		DATE
LOCATION		
KART NUMBER		/ /

RACE NUMBER IN ROW		CURRENT STANDING	
WEATHER CONDITION	☀ ☁ ❄ ⚡ 〜	TIME OF YEAR	🌷 ☀ 🍃 ❄
TIRES USED	⚙	RACE START	🕐
		RACE FINISH	
ENGINE SIZE	⚙	FINISHING POSITION	🏁

TYRE PRESSURE		START POSITION
FRONT	REAR	
		LAPS COMPLETED
		1ST ROUND AT

FASTEST TIME	FASTEST LAP

FURTHER OBSERVATIONS

RACE EVENT		DATE
LOCATION		
KART NUMBER		/ /

RACE NUMBER IN ROW		CURRENT STANDING	
WEATHER CONDITION	☀ ☁ ❄ ⚡ 🌬	TIME OF YEAR	🌷 ☀ 🍂 ❄
TIRES USED	⊚	RACE START	🕐
		RACE FINISH	
ENGINE SIZE	🔧	FINISHING POSITION	🏁

TYRE PRESSURE		START POSITION
FRONT	REAR	
		LAPS COMPLETED
		1ST ROUND AT

FASTEST TIME	FASTEST LAP

FURTHER OBSERVATIONS

RACE EVENT		DATE
LOCATION		
KART NUMBER		/ /

RACE NUMBER IN ROW		CURRENT STANDING	
WEATHER CONDITION	☀ ☁ ❄ ⛈ 🌬	TIME OF YEAR	🌷 ☀ 🍂 ❄
TIRES USED	⊙	RACE START	🕐
		RACE FINISH	
ENGINE SIZE	⚙	FINISHING POSITION	🏁

TYRE PRESSURE		START POSITION
FRONT	REAR	
		LAPS COMPLETED
		1ST ROUND AT

FASTEST TIME	FASTEST LAP

FURTHER OBSERVATIONS

RACE EVENT		DATE
LOCATION		
KART NUMBER		/ /

RACE NUMBER IN ROW		CURRENT STANDING	
WEATHER CONDITION	☀ ☁ ❄ ⛈ 〰	TIME OF YEAR	🌷 ☀ 🍂 ❄
TIRES USED	⊚	RACE START	🕐
		RACE FINISH	
ENGINE SIZE	⚙	FINISHING POSITION	🏁

TYRE PRESSURE		START POSITION
FRONT	REAR	
		LAPS COMPLETED
		1ST ROUND AT

FASTEST TIME	FASTEST LAP

FURTHER OBSERVATIONS

RACE EVENT		DATE
LOCATION		
KART NUMBER		/ /

RACE NUMBER IN ROW		CURRENT STANDING	
WEATHER CONDITION	☀ ☁ ❄ ⛈ 🌬	TIME OF YEAR	🌷 ☀ 🍃 ❄
TIRES USED	⚙	RACE START	🕐
		RACE FINISH	
ENGINE SIZE	🔧	FINISHING POSITION	🏁

TYRE PRESSURE		START POSITION
FRONT	REAR	
		LAPS COMPLETED
		1ST ROUND AT

FASTEST TIME	FASTEST LAP

FURTHER OBSERVATIONS

RACE EVENT			DATE
LOCATION			
KART NUMBER			/ /

RACE NUMBER IN ROW		CURRENT STANDING	
WEATHER CONDITION	☀ ☁ ❄ ⛈ 🌬	TIME OF YEAR	🌷 ☀ 🍁 ❄
TIRES USED	◎	RACE START	🕐
		RACE FINISH	
ENGINE SIZE	🔧	FINISHING POSITION	🏁

TYRE PRESSURE		START POSITION
FRONT	REAR	
		LAPS COMPLETED
		1ST ROUND AT

FASTEST TIME	FASTEST LAP

FURTHER OBSERVATIONS

RACE EVENT		DATE
LOCATION		
KART NUMBER		/ /

RACE NUMBER IN ROW		CURRENT STANDING	
WEATHER CONDITION	☀ ☁ ❄ ⚡ 🌬	TIME OF YEAR	🌷 ☀ 🍁 ❄
TIRES USED	◉	RACE START	🕐
		RACE FINISH	
ENGINE SIZE	🔧	FINISHING POSITION	🏁

TYRE PRESSURE		START POSITION
FRONT	REAR	
		LAPS COMPLETED
		1ST ROUND AT

FASTEST TIME	FASTEST LAP

FURTHER OBSERVATIONS

RACE EVENT		DATE
LOCATION		
KART NUMBER		/ /

RACE NUMBER IN ROW		CURRENT STANDING	
WEATHER CONDITION	☀ ☔ ❄ ⛈ 🌬	TIME OF YEAR	🌷 ☀ 🍃 ❄
TIRES USED	⚙	RACE START RACE FINISH	🕐
ENGINE SIZE		FINISHING POSITION	🏁

TYRE PRESSURE		START POSITION
FRONT	REAR	
		LAPS COMPLETED
		1ST ROUND AT

FASTEST TIME	FASTEST LAP

FURTHER OBSERVATIONS

RACE EVENT		DATE
LOCATION		
KART NUMBER		/ /

RACE NUMBER IN ROW		CURRENT STANDING	
WEATHER CONDITION	☀ ☁ ❄ ⛈ 〰	TIME OF YEAR	🌷 ☀ 🍂 ❄
TIRES USED	⊛	RACE START	🕐
		RACE FINISH	
ENGINE SIZE	🔧	FINISHING POSITION	🏁

TYRE PRESSURE		START POSITION
FRONT	REAR	
		LAPS COMPLETED
		1ST ROUND AT

FASTEST TIME	FASTEST LAP

FURTHER OBSERVATIONS

RACE EVENT		DATE
LOCATION		
KART NUMBER		/ /

RACE NUMBER IN ROW		CURRENT STANDING	
WEATHER CONDITION	☀ ☁ ❄ ⚡ 🌬	TIME OF YEAR	🌷 ☀ 🍂 ❄
TIRES USED	⚙	RACE START	🕐
		RACE FINISH	
ENGINE SIZE		FINISHING POSITION	🏁

TYRE PRESSURE		START POSITION
FRONT	REAR	
		LAPS COMPLETED
		1ST ROUND AT

FASTEST TIME	FASTEST LAP

FURTHER OBSERVATIONS

RACE EVENT		DATE
LOCATION		
KART NUMBER		/ /

RACE NUMBER IN ROW			CURRENT STANDING	
WEATHER CONDITION	☀ ☁ ❄ ⛈ 🌬		TIME OF YEAR	🌷 ☀ 🍃 ❄
TIRES USED	⚙		RACE START	🕐
			RACE FINISH	
ENGINE SIZE	🔧		FINISHING POSITION	🏁

TYRE PRESSURE

FRONT	REAR

START POSITION

LAPS COMPLETED

1ST ROUND AT

FASTEST TIME	FASTEST LAP

FURTHER OBSERVATIONS

RACE EVENT		DATE
LOCATION		
KART NUMBER		/ /

RACE NUMBER IN ROW		CURRENT STANDING	
WEATHER CONDITION	☀ ☁ ❄ ⛈ 🌬	TIME OF YEAR	🌷 ☀ 🍂 ❄
TIRES USED	⚙	RACE START	🕐
		RACE FINISH	
ENGINE SIZE	🔧	FINISHING POSITION	🏁

TYRE PRESSURE		START POSITION
FRONT	REAR	
		LAPS COMPLETED
		1ST ROUND AT

FASTEST TIME	FASTEST LAP

FURTHER OBSERVATIONS

RACE EVENT		DATE
LOCATION		
KART NUMBER		/ /

RACE NUMBER IN ROW		CURRENT STANDING	
WEATHER CONDITION	☀ ☁ ❄ ⛈ 🌬	TIME OF YEAR	🌷 ☀ 🍃 ❄
TIRES USED	⚙	RACE START	🕐
		RACE FINISH	
ENGINE SIZE	🔧	FINISHING POSITION	🏁

TYRE PRESSURE		START POSITION
FRONT	REAR	
		LAPS COMPLETED
		1ST ROUND AT

FASTEST TIME	FASTEST LAP

FURTHER OBSERVATIONS

RACE EVENT		DATE
LOCATION		
KART NUMBER		/ /

RACE NUMBER IN ROW		CURRENT STANDING	
WEATHER CONDITION	☀ ☁ ❄ ⛈ 💨	TIME OF YEAR	🌷 ☀ 🍂 ❄
TIRES USED	◎	RACE START	🕐
		RACE FINISH	
ENGINE SIZE	🔧	FINISHING POSITION	🏁

TYRE PRESSURE

START POSITION

FRONT	REAR

LAPS COMPLETED

1ST ROUND AT

FASTEST TIME

FASTEST LAP

FURTHER OBSERVATIONS

RACE EVENT			DATE
LOCATION			
KART NUMBER			/ /

RACE NUMBER IN ROW		CURRENT STANDING	
WEATHER CONDITION	☀ ☁ ❄ ⚡ 🌬	TIME OF YEAR	🌷 ☀ 🍃 ❄
TIRES USED	⚙	RACE START	🕐
		RACE FINISH	
ENGINE SIZE	🔧	FINISHING POSITION	🏁

TYRE PRESSURE		START POSITION
FRONT	REAR	
		LAPS COMPLETED
		1ST ROUND AT

FASTEST TIME	FASTEST LAP

FURTHER OBSERVATIONS

RACE EVENT		DATE
LOCATION		
KART NUMBER		/ /

RACE NUMBER IN ROW		CURRENT STANDING	
WEATHER CONDITION	☀ ☁ ❄ ⚡ 🌬	TIME OF YEAR	🌷 ☀ 🍂 ❄
TIRES USED	⊕	RACE START	🕐
		RACE FINISH	
ENGINE SIZE	🔧	FINISHING POSITION	🏁

TYRE PRESSURE   START POSITION

FRONT	REAR	
		LAPS COMPLETED
		1ST ROUND AT

FASTEST TIME   FASTEST LAP

FURTHER OBSERVATIONS

RACE EVENT		DATE
LOCATION		
KART NUMBER		/ /

RACE NUMBER IN ROW		CURRENT STANDING	
WEATHER CONDITION	☀ ☁ ❄ ⛈ 〜	TIME OF YEAR	🌷 ☀ 🍃 ❄
TIRES USED	⚙	RACE START	🕐
		RACE FINISH	
ENGINE SIZE	🔧	FINISHING POSITION	🏁

TYRE PRESSURE		START POSITION
FRONT	REAR	
		LAPS COMPLETED
		1ST ROUND AT

FASTEST TIME	FASTEST LAP

FURTHER OBSERVATIONS

RACE EVENT		DATE
LOCATION		
KART NUMBER		/ /

RACE NUMBER IN ROW		CURRENT STANDING	
WEATHER CONDITION	☀ ☁ ❄ ⚡ 🌬	TIME OF YEAR	🌷 ☀ 🍂 ❄
TIRES USED	⊚	RACE START	🕐
		RACE FINISH	
ENGINE SIZE	🔧	FINISHING POSITION	🏁

TYRE PRESSURE		START POSITION
FRONT	REAR	
		LAPS COMPLETED
		1ST ROUND AT

FASTEST TIME	FASTEST LAP

FURTHER OBSERVATIONS

RACE EVENT		DATE
LOCATION		
KART NUMBER		/ /

RACE NUMBER IN ROW			CURRENT STANDING	
WEATHER CONDITION	☀ ☁ ❄ ⚡ 🌬		TIME OF YEAR	🌷 ☀ 🍃 ❄
TIRES USED	⊛		RACE START	⏱
			RACE FINISH	
ENGINE SIZE	🔧		FINISHING POSITION	🏁

TYRE PRESSURE		START POSITION
FRONT	**REAR**	
		LAPS COMPLETED
		1ST ROUND AT

FASTEST TIME	FASTEST LAP

FURTHER OBSERVATIONS

RACE EVENT		DATE
LOCATION		
KART NUMBER		/ /

RACE NUMBER IN ROW		CURRENT STANDING	
WEATHER CONDITION	☀ ☁ ❄ ⛈ 🌬	TIME OF YEAR	🌷 ☀ 🍃 ❄
TIRES USED	⚙	RACE START	🕐
		RACE FINISH	
ENGINE SIZE		FINISHING POSITION	🏁

TYRE PRESSURE		START POSITION
FRONT	REAR	

LAPS COMPLETED

1ST ROUND AT

FASTEST TIME	FASTEST LAP

FURTHER OBSERVATIONS

RACE EVENT		DATE
LOCATION		
KART NUMBER		/ /

RACE NUMBER IN ROW		CURRENT STANDING	
WEATHER CONDITION	☀ ☁ ❄ ⛈ 🌬	TIME OF YEAR	🌷 ☀ 🍁 ❄
TIRES USED	⚙	RACE START	🕐
		RACE FINISH	
ENGINE SIZE	⚙	FINISHING POSITION	🏁

TYRE PRESSURE		START POSITION
FRONT	REAR	
		LAPS COMPLETED
		1ST ROUND AT

FASTEST TIME	FASTEST LAP

FURTHER OBSERVATIONS

RACE EVENT		DATE
LOCATION		
KART NUMBER		/ /

RACE NUMBER IN ROW		CURRENT STANDING	
WEATHER CONDITION	☀ ☁ ❄ ⛈ 🌬	TIME OF YEAR	🌷 ☀ 🍃 ❄
TIRES USED	◉	RACE START	🕐
		RACE FINISH	
ENGINE SIZE	⚙	FINISHING POSITION	🏁

TYRE PRESSURE		START POSITION
FRONT	REAR	
		LAPS COMPLETED
		1ST ROUND AT

FASTEST TIME	FASTEST LAP

FURTHER OBSERVATIONS

RACE EVENT		DATE
LOCATION		
KART NUMBER		/ /

RACE NUMBER IN ROW		CURRENT STANDING	
WEATHER CONDITION	☀ ☁ ❄ ⛆ 🌬	TIME OF YEAR	🌷 ☀ 🍃 ❄
TIRES USED	⚙	RACE START	🕐
		RACE FINISH	
ENGINE SIZE	🔧	FINISHING POSITION	🏁

TYRE PRESSURE		START POSITION
FRONT	REAR	
		LAPS COMPLETED
		1ST ROUND AT

FASTEST TIME	FASTEST LAP

FURTHER OBSERVATIONS

RACE EVENT		DATE
LOCATION		
KART NUMBER		/ /

RACE NUMBER IN ROW		CURRENT STANDING	
WEATHER CONDITION	☀ ☁ ❄ ⚡ 〰	TIME OF YEAR	🌷 ☀ 🍃 ❄
TIRES USED	⊚	RACE START RACE FINISH	🕐
ENGINE SIZE	🔧	FINISHING POSITION	🏁

TYRE PRESSURE		START POSITION
FRONT	REAR	
		LAPS COMPLETED
		1ST ROUND AT

FASTEST TIME	FASTEST LAP

FURTHER OBSERVATIONS

RACE EVENT		DATE
LOCATION		
KART NUMBER		/ /

RACE NUMBER IN ROW		CURRENT STANDING	
WEATHER CONDITION	☀ ☁ ❄ ⛈ 🌬	TIME OF YEAR	🌷 ☀ 🍃 ❄
TIRES USED	⊕	RACE START	🕐
		RACE FINISH	
ENGINE SIZE		FINISHING POSITION	🏁

TYRE PRESSURE		START POSITION
FRONT	REAR	
		LAPS COMPLETED
		1ST ROUND AT

FASTEST TIME	FASTEST LAP

FURTHER OBSERVATIONS

RACE EVENT		DATE
LOCATION		
KART NUMBER		/ /

RACE NUMBER IN ROW		CURRENT STANDING	
WEATHER CONDITION	☀ ☂ ❄ ⚡ 🌬	TIME OF YEAR	🌷 ☀ 🍂 ❄
TIRES USED	⚙	RACE START	🕐
		RACE FINISH	
ENGINE SIZE		FINISHING POSITION	🏁

TYRE PRESSURE		START POSITION
FRONT	REAR	
		LAPS COMPLETED
		1ST ROUND AT

FASTEST TIME	FASTEST LAP

FURTHER OBSERVATIONS

RACE EVENT		DATE
LOCATION		
KART NUMBER		/ /

RACE NUMBER IN ROW		CURRENT STANDING	
WEATHER CONDITION	☀ ☁ ❄ ⛈ 🌬	TIME OF YEAR	🌷 ☀ 🍃 ❄
TIRES USED	◉	RACE START	🕐
		RACE FINISH	
ENGINE SIZE	🔧	FINISHING POSITION	🏁

TYRE PRESSURE		START POSITION
FRONT	REAR	
		LAPS COMPLETED
		1ST ROUND AT

FASTEST TIME	FASTEST LAP

FURTHER OBSERVATIONS

RACE EVENT		DATE
LOCATION		
KART NUMBER		/ /

RACE NUMBER IN ROW		CURRENT STANDING	
WEATHER CONDITION	☀ ☁ ❄ ⛈ 💨	TIME OF YEAR	🌷 ☀ 🍃 ❄
TIRES USED	⊕	RACE START	🕐
		RACE FINISH	
ENGINE SIZE	⚙	FINISHING POSITION	🏁

TYRE PRESSURE		START POSITION
FRONT	REAR	
		LAPS COMPLETED
		1ST ROUND AT

FASTEST TIME	FASTEST LAP

FURTHER OBSERVATIONS

RACE EVENT		DATE
LOCATION		
KART NUMBER		/ /

RACE NUMBER IN ROW		CURRENT STANDING	
WEATHER CONDITION	☀ ☁ ❄ ⛈ 💨	TIME OF YEAR	🌷 ☀ 🍁 ❄
TIRES USED	⚙	RACE START	🕐
		RACE FINISH	
ENGINE SIZE	🔧	FINISHING POSITION	🏁

TYRE PRESSURE		START POSITION
FRONT	REAR	
		LAPS COMPLETED
		1ST ROUND AT

FASTEST TIME	FASTEST LAP

FURTHER OBSERVATIONS

RACE EVENT		DATE
LOCATION		
KART NUMBER		/ /

RACE NUMBER IN ROW		CURRENT STANDING	
WEATHER CONDITION	☀ ☁ ❄ ⛈ ꞈ	TIME OF YEAR	🌷 ☀ 🍃 ❄
TIRES USED	⊛	RACE START	🕐
		RACE FINISH	
ENGINE SIZE	🔧	FINISHING POSITION	🏁

TYRE PRESSURE		START POSITION
FRONT	REAR	
		LAPS COMPLETED
		1ST ROUND AT

FASTEST TIME	FASTEST LAP

FURTHER OBSERVATIONS

RACE EVENT		DATE
LOCATION		
KART NUMBER		/ /

RACE NUMBER IN ROW		CURRENT STANDING	
WEATHER CONDITION	☀ ☁ ❄ ⚡ 💨	TIME OF YEAR	🌷 ☀ 🍃 ❄
TIRES USED	⚙	RACE START	🕐
		RACE FINISH	
ENGINE SIZE	🔧	FINISHING POSITION	🏁

TYRE PRESSURE		START POSITION
FRONT	REAR	
		LAPS COMPLETED
		1ST ROUND AT

FASTEST TIME	FASTEST LAP

FURTHER OBSERVATIONS

RACE EVENT		DATE
LOCATION		
KART NUMBER		/ /

RACE NUMBER IN ROW		CURRENT STANDING	
WEATHER CONDITION	☀ ☁ ❄ ⚡ 🌬	TIME OF YEAR	🌷 ☀ 🍃 ❄
TIRES USED	⊚	RACE START	🕐
		RACE FINISH	
ENGINE SIZE	🔧	FINISHING POSITION	🏁

TYRE PRESSURE		START POSITION
FRONT	REAR	
		LAPS COMPLETED
		1ST ROUND AT

FASTEST TIME	FASTEST LAP

FURTHER OBSERVATIONS

RACE EVENT		DATE
LOCATION		
KART NUMBER		/ /

RACE NUMBER IN ROW		CURRENT STANDING	
WEATHER CONDITION	☀ ☁ ❄ ⛈ 🌬	TIME OF YEAR	🌷 ☀ 🍁 ❄
TIRES USED	◉	RACE START	🕐
		RACE FINISH	
ENGINE SIZE	⚙	FINISHING POSITION	🏁

TYRE PRESSURE		START POSITION
FRONT	REAR	
		LAPS COMPLETED
		1ST ROUND AT

FASTEST TIME	FASTEST LAP

FURTHER OBSERVATIONS

RACE EVENT		DATE
LOCATION		
KART NUMBER		/ /

RACE NUMBER IN ROW		CURRENT STANDING	
WEATHER CONDITION	☼ ☁ ❄ ⛈ 〰	TIME OF YEAR	❀ ☼ 🍃 ❄
TIRES USED	◉	RACE START	⊕
		RACE FINISH	
ENGINE SIZE	🔧	FINISHING POSITION	🏁

TYRE PRESSURE		START POSITION
FRONT	REAR	
		LAPS COMPLETED
		1ST ROUND AT

FASTEST TIME	FASTEST LAP

FURTHER OBSERVATIONS

RACE EVENT		DATE
LOCATION		
KART NUMBER		/ /

RACE NUMBER IN ROW		CURRENT STANDING	
WEATHER CONDITION	☀ ☔ ❄ ⚡ 💨	TIME OF YEAR	🌷 ☀ 🍂 ❄
TIRES USED	⬤	RACE START	🕐
		RACE FINISH	
ENGINE SIZE	🔧	FINISHING POSITION	🏁

TYRE PRESSURE		START POSITION
FRONT	REAR	
		LAPS COMPLETED
		1ST ROUND AT

FASTEST TIME	FASTEST LAP

FURTHER OBSERVATIONS

RACE EVENT		DATE
LOCATION		
KART NUMBER		/ /

RACE NUMBER IN ROW		CURRENT STANDING	
WEATHER CONDITION	☀ ☁ ❄ ⚡ 〰	TIME OF YEAR	🌷 ☀ 🍃 ❄
TIRES USED	◉	RACE START	🕐
		RACE FINISH	
ENGINE SIZE	⚙	FINISHING POSITION	🏁

TYRE PRESSURE		START POSITION
FRONT	REAR	
		LAPS COMPLETED
		1ST ROUND AT

FASTEST TIME	FASTEST LAP

FURTHER OBSERVATIONS

RACE EVENT		DATE
LOCATION		
KART NUMBER		/ /

RACE NUMBER IN ROW		CURRENT STANDING	
WEATHER CONDITION	☀ ☁ ❄ ⛈ 🌬	TIME OF YEAR	🌷 ☀ 🍂 ❄
TIRES USED	⊚	RACE START	🕐
		RACE FINISH	
ENGINE SIZE	⚙	FINISHING POSITION	🏁

TYRE PRESSURE		START POSITION
FRONT	REAR	
		LAPS COMPLETED
		1ST ROUND AT

FASTEST TIME	FASTEST LAP

FURTHER OBSERVATIONS

RACE EVENT		DATE
LOCATION		
KART NUMBER		/ /

RACE NUMBER IN ROW		CURRENT STANDING	
WEATHER CONDITION	☀ ☁ ❄ ⛈ 💨	TIME OF YEAR	🌷 ☀ 🍂 ❄
TIRES USED	⚙	RACE START	🕐
		RACE FINISH	
ENGINE SIZE	🔧	FINISHING POSITION	🏁

TYRE PRESSURE		START POSITION
FRONT	REAR	
		LAPS COMPLETED
		1ST ROUND AT

FASTEST TIME	FASTEST LAP

FURTHER OBSERVATIONS

RACE EVENT		DATE
LOCATION		
KART NUMBER		/ /

RACE NUMBER IN ROW		CURRENT STANDING	
WEATHER CONDITION	☀ ☁ ❄ ⛈ 🌬	TIME OF YEAR	🌷 ☀ 🍂 ❄
TIRES USED	⚙	RACE START	🕐
		RACE FINISH	
ENGINE SIZE	⚙	FINISHING POSITION	🏁

TYRE PRESSURE		START POSITION
FRONT	REAR	
		LAPS COMPLETED
		1ST ROUND AT

FASTEST TIME	FASTEST LAP

FURTHER OBSERVATIONS

RACE EVENT		DATE
LOCATION		
KART NUMBER		/ /

RACE NUMBER IN ROW		CURRENT STANDING	
WEATHER CONDITION	☀ ☁ ❄ ⛈ 🌬	TIME OF YEAR	🌷 ☀ 🍃 ❄
TIRES USED	⚙	RACE START	🕐
		RACE FINISH	
ENGINE SIZE	🔧	FINISHING POSITION	🏁

TYRE PRESSURE		START POSITION
FRONT	REAR	
		LAPS COMPLETED
		1ST ROUND AT

FASTEST TIME	FASTEST LAP

FURTHER OBSERVATIONS

RACE EVENT		DATE
LOCATION		
KART NUMBER		/ /

RACE NUMBER IN ROW		CURRENT STANDING	
WEATHER CONDITION	☀ ☁ ❄ ⛈ 💨	TIME OF YEAR	🌷 ☀ 🍂 ❄
TIRES USED	⚙	RACE START	🕐
		RACE FINISH	
ENGINE SIZE	⚙	FINISHING POSITION	🏁

TYRE PRESSURE		START POSITION
FRONT	REAR	
		LAPS COMPLETED
		1ST ROUND AT

FASTEST TIME	FASTEST LAP

FURTHER OBSERVATIONS

RACE EVENT		DATE
LOCATION		
KART NUMBER		/ /

RACE NUMBER IN ROW		CURRENT STANDING	
WEATHER CONDITION	☀ ☁ ❄ ⚡ 〰	TIME OF YEAR	🌷 ☀ 🍁 ❄
TIRES USED	⊚	RACE START	🕐
		RACE FINISH	
ENGINE SIZE	🔧	FINISHING POSITION	🏁

TYRE PRESSURE		START POSITION
FRONT	REAR	
		LAPS COMPLETED
		1ST ROUND AT

FASTEST TIME	FASTEST LAP

FURTHER OBSERVATIONS

RACE EVENT		DATE
LOCATION		
KART NUMBER		/ /

RACE NUMBER IN ROW		CURRENT STANDING	
WEATHER CONDITION	☀ ☁ ❄ ⚡ 💨	TIME OF YEAR	🌷 ☀ 🍂 ❄
TIRES USED	⊚	RACE START	🕐
		RACE FINISH	
ENGINE SIZE		FINISHING POSITION	🏁

TYRE PRESSURE		START POSITION
FRONT	REAR	
		LAPS COMPLETED
		1ST ROUND AT

FASTEST TIME	FASTEST LAP

FURTHER OBSERVATIONS

RACE EVENT		DATE
LOCATION		
KART NUMBER		/ /

RACE NUMBER IN ROW		CURRENT STANDING	
WEATHER CONDITION	☀ ☁ ❄ ⚡ 🍃	TIME OF YEAR	🌷 ☀ 🍂 ❄
TIRES USED	⚙	RACE START	🕐
		RACE FINISH	
ENGINE SIZE	🔧	FINISHING POSITION	🏁

TYRE PRESSURE		START POSITION
FRONT	REAR	
		LAPS COMPLETED
		1ST ROUND AT

FASTEST TIME	FASTEST LAP

FURTHER OBSERVATIONS

RACE EVENT		DATE
LOCATION		
KART NUMBER		/ /

RACE NUMBER IN ROW		CURRENT STANDING	
WEATHER CONDITION	☀ ☁ ❄ ⛈ 🌬	TIME OF YEAR	🌷 ☀ 🍂 ❄
TIRES USED	⊚	RACE START	🕐
		RACE FINISH	
ENGINE SIZE	🔧	FINISHING POSITION	🏁

TYRE PRESSURE		START POSITION

FRONT	REAR	
		LAPS COMPLETED
		1ST ROUND AT

FASTEST TIME	FASTEST LAP

FURTHER OBSERVATIONS

RACE EVENT		DATE	
LOCATION			
KART NUMBER		/ /	

RACE NUMBER IN ROW		CURRENT STANDING	
WEATHER CONDITION	☀ ☁ ❄ ⚡ 〜	TIME OF YEAR	🌷 ☀ 🍃 ❄
TIRES USED	⚙	RACE START	🕐
		RACE FINISH	
ENGINE SIZE	🔧	FINISHING POSITION	🏁

TYRE PRESSURE		START POSITION
FRONT	REAR	
		LAPS COMPLETED
		1ST ROUND AT

FASTEST TIME	FASTEST LAP

FURTHER OBSERVATIONS

RACE EVENT		DATE
LOCATION		
KART NUMBER		/ /

RACE NUMBER IN ROW		CURRENT STANDING	
WEATHER CONDITION	☀ ☁ ❄ ⛈ 〰	TIME OF YEAR	🌷 ☀ 🍂 ❄
TIRES USED	⚙	RACE START	🕐
		RACE FINISH	
ENGINE SIZE	⚙	FINISHING POSITION	🏁

TYRE PRESSURE		START POSITION
FRONT	REAR	
		LAPS COMPLETED
		1ST ROUND AT

FASTEST TIME	FASTEST LAP

FURTHER OBSERVATIONS

RACE EVENT		DATE	
LOCATION			
KART NUMBER		/ /	

RACE NUMBER IN ROW		CURRENT STANDING	
WEATHER CONDITION	☀ ☔ ❄ ⛈ 〰	TIME OF YEAR	🌷 ☀ 🍃 ❄
TIRES USED	◉	RACE START	🕐
		RACE FINISH	
ENGINE SIZE	🔧	FINISHING POSITION	🏁

TYRE PRESSURE

FRONT	REAR

START POSITION

LAPS COMPLETED

1ST ROUND AT

FASTEST TIME	FASTEST LAP

FURTHER OBSERVATIONS

RACE EVENT		DATE
LOCATION		
KART NUMBER		/ /

RACE NUMBER IN ROW		CURRENT STANDING	
WEATHER CONDITION	☀ ☁ ❄ ⛈ 💨	TIME OF YEAR	🌷 ☀ 🍂 ❄
TIRES USED	⊙	RACE START	🕐
		RACE FINISH	
ENGINE SIZE	⚙	FINISHING POSITION	🏁

TYRE PRESSURE		START POSITION
FRONT	REAR	
		LAPS COMPLETED
		1ST ROUND AT

FASTEST TIME	FASTEST LAP

FURTHER OBSERVATIONS

RACE EVENT		DATE
LOCATION		
KART NUMBER		/ /

RACE NUMBER IN ROW		CURRENT STANDING	
WEATHER CONDITION	☀ ☁ ❄ ⛈ 💨	TIME OF YEAR	🌷 ☀ 🍁 ❄
TIRES USED	⚙	RACE START	🕐
		RACE FINISH	
ENGINE SIZE		FINISHING POSITION	🏁

TYRE PRESSURE		START POSITION
FRONT	REAR	
		LAPS COMPLETED
		1ST ROUND AT

FASTEST TIME	FASTEST LAP

FURTHER OBSERVATIONS

RACE EVENT		DATE
LOCATION		
KART NUMBER		/ /

RACE NUMBER IN ROW		CURRENT STANDING	
WEATHER CONDITION	☀ ☁ ❄ ⚡ 💨	TIME OF YEAR	🌷 ☀ 🍃 ❄
TIRES USED	⚙	RACE START	🕐
		RACE FINISH	
ENGINE SIZE		FINISHING POSITION	🏁

TYRE PRESSURE		START POSITION
FRONT	REAR	
		LAPS COMPLETED
		1ST ROUND AT

FASTEST TIME	FASTEST LAP

FURTHER OBSERVATIONS

RACE EVENT		DATE
LOCATION		
KART NUMBER		/ /

RACE NUMBER IN ROW		CURRENT STANDING	
WEATHER CONDITION	☀ ☁ ❄ ⛈ 🌬	TIME OF YEAR	🌷 ☀ 🍃 ❄
TIRES USED	⚙	RACE START	🕐
		RACE FINISH	
ENGINE SIZE	🔧	FINISHING POSITION	🏁

TYRE PRESSURE		START POSITION
FRONT	REAR	
		LAPS COMPLETED
		1ST ROUND AT

FASTEST TIME	FASTEST LAP

FURTHER OBSERVATIONS

RACE EVENT		DATE
LOCATION		
KART NUMBER		/ /

RACE NUMBER IN ROW		CURRENT STANDING	
WEATHER CONDITION	☀ ☁ ❄ ⛈ 🌬	TIME OF YEAR	🌷 ☀ 🍂 ❄
TIRES USED	◉	RACE START	🕐
		RACE FINISH	
ENGINE SIZE	⚙	FINISHING POSITION	🏁

TYRE PRESSURE		START POSITION
FRONT	REAR	
		LAPS COMPLETED
		1ST ROUND AT

FASTEST TIME	FASTEST LAP

FURTHER OBSERVATIONS

RACE EVENT		DATE
LOCATION		
KART NUMBER		/ /

RACE NUMBER IN ROW		CURRENT STANDING	
WEATHER CONDITION	☀ ☁ ❄ ⚡ ≈	TIME OF YEAR	🌷 ☀ 🍃 ❄
TIRES USED	◉	RACE START	🕐
		RACE FINISH	
ENGINE SIZE	🔧	FINISHING POSITION	🏁

TYRE PRESSURE		START POSITION
FRONT	REAR	
		LAPS COMPLETED
		1ST ROUND AT

FASTEST TIME	FASTEST LAP

FURTHER OBSERVATIONS

RACE EVENT		DATE
LOCATION		
KART NUMBER		/ /

RACE NUMBER IN ROW		CURRENT STANDING	
WEATHER CONDITION	☀ ☁ ❄ ⚡ 🌬	TIME OF YEAR	🌷 ☀ 🍃 ❄
TIRES USED	⊕	RACE START	🕐
		RACE FINISH	
ENGINE SIZE		FINISHING POSITION	🏁

TYRE PRESSURE		START POSITION
FRONT	REAR	
		LAPS COMPLETED
		1ST ROUND AT

FASTEST TIME	FASTEST LAP

FURTHER OBSERVATIONS

RACE EVENT		DATE
LOCATION		
KART NUMBER		/ /

RACE NUMBER IN ROW		CURRENT STANDING	
WEATHER CONDITION	☀ ☁ ❄ ⛈ ➰	TIME OF YEAR	🌷 ☀ 🍃 ❄
TIRES USED	⊚	RACE START	🕐
		RACE FINISH	
ENGINE SIZE		FINISHING POSITION	🏁

TYRE PRESSURE		START POSITION
FRONT	REAR	
		LAPS COMPLETED
		1ST ROUND AT

FASTEST TIME	FASTEST LAP

FURTHER OBSERVATIONS

RACE EVENT		DATE
LOCATION		
KART NUMBER		/ /

RACE NUMBER IN ROW		CURRENT STANDING	
WEATHER CONDITION	☀ ☁ ❄ ⛈ 🌬	TIME OF YEAR	🌷 ☀ 🍂 ❄
TIRES USED	◉	RACE START	🕐
		RACE FINISH	
ENGINE SIZE	⚙	FINISHING POSITION	🏁

TYRE PRESSURE		START POSITION
FRONT	REAR	
		LAPS COMPLETED
		1ST ROUND AT

FASTEST TIME	FASTEST LAP

FURTHER OBSERVATIONS

RACE EVENT		DATE
LOCATION		
KART NUMBER		/ /

RACE NUMBER IN ROW		CURRENT STANDING	
WEATHER CONDITION	☀ ☔ ❄ ⚡ 🌬	TIME OF YEAR	🌷 ☀ 🍂 ❄
TIRES USED	⊚	RACE START	🕐
		RACE FINISH	
ENGINE SIZE	🔧	FINISHING POSITION	🏁

TYRE PRESSURE		START POSITION
FRONT	REAR	
		LAPS COMPLETED
		1ST ROUND AT

FASTEST TIME	FASTEST LAP

FURTHER OBSERVATIONS

RACE EVENT		DATE
LOCATION		
KART NUMBER		/ /

RACE NUMBER IN ROW		CURRENT STANDING	
WEATHER CONDITION	☀ ☁ ❄ ⚡ 💨	TIME OF YEAR	🌷 ☀ 🍁 ❄
TIRES USED	⚙	RACE START	🕐
		RACE FINISH	
ENGINE SIZE	🔧	FINISHING POSITION	🏁

TYRE PRESSURE		START POSITION
FRONT	REAR	
		LAPS COMPLETED
		1ST ROUND AT

FASTEST TIME	FASTEST LAP

FURTHER OBSERVATIONS

RACE EVENT		DATE
LOCATION		
KART NUMBER		/ /

RACE NUMBER IN ROW		CURRENT STANDING	
WEATHER CONDITION	☀ ☁ ❄ ⛈ 🌬	TIME OF YEAR	🌷 ☀ 🍂 ❄
TIRES USED	⊚	RACE START	🕐
		RACE FINISH	
ENGINE SIZE	🔧	FINISHING POSITION	🏁

TYRE PRESSURE		START POSITION
FRONT	REAR	
		LAPS COMPLETED
		1ST ROUND AT

FASTEST TIME	FASTEST LAP

FURTHER OBSERVATIONS

RACE EVENT		DATE
LOCATION		
KART NUMBER		/ /

RACE NUMBER IN ROW		CURRENT STANDING	
WEATHER CONDITION	☀ ☁ ❄ ⛈ 🌬	TIME OF YEAR	🌷 ☀ 🍁 ❄
TIRES USED	⊚	RACE START	🕐
		RACE FINISH	
ENGINE SIZE	⚙	FINISHING POSITION	🏁

TYRE PRESSURE		START POSITION

FRONT	REAR	
		LAPS COMPLETED
		1ST ROUND AT

FASTEST TIME	FASTEST LAP

FURTHER OBSERVATIONS

RACE EVENT		DATE
LOCATION		
KART NUMBER		/ /

RACE NUMBER IN ROW		CURRENT STANDING	
WEATHER CONDITION	☀ ☁ ❄ ⚡ 〰	TIME OF YEAR	🌷 ☀ 🍂 ❄
TIRES USED	⚙	RACE START	🕐
		RACE FINISH	
ENGINE SIZE	🔧	FINISHING POSITION	🏁

TYRE PRESSURE		START POSITION
FRONT	REAR	
		LAPS COMPLETED
		1ST ROUND AT

FASTEST TIME	FASTEST LAP

FURTHER OBSERVATIONS

RACE EVENT		DATE
LOCATION		
KART NUMBER		/ /

RACE NUMBER IN ROW		CURRENT STANDING	
WEATHER CONDITION	☀ ☁ ❄ ⚡ 💨	TIME OF YEAR	🌷 ☀ 🍂 ❄
TIRES USED	⚙	RACE START	🕐
		RACE FINISH	
ENGINE SIZE	🔧	FINISHING POSITION	🏁

TYRE PRESSURE		START POSITION
FRONT	REAR	
		LAPS COMPLETED
		1ST ROUND AT

FASTEST TIME	FASTEST LAP

FURTHER OBSERVATIONS

RACE EVENT		DATE
LOCATION		
KART NUMBER		/ /

RACE NUMBER IN ROW		CURRENT STANDING	
WEATHER CONDITION	☀ ☁ ❄ ⚡ 〰	TIME OF YEAR	🌷 ☀ 🍃 ❄
TIRES USED	⊚	RACE START	🕐
		RACE FINISH	
ENGINE SIZE	🔧	FINISHING POSITION	🏁

TYRE PRESSURE		START POSITION
FRONT	REAR	
		LAPS COMPLETED
		1ST ROUND AT

FASTEST TIME	FASTEST LAP

FURTHER OBSERVATIONS

RACE EVENT		DATE
LOCATION		
KART NUMBER		/ /

RACE NUMBER IN ROW		CURRENT STANDING	
WEATHER CONDITION	☀ ☁ ❄ ⛈ 💨	TIME OF YEAR	🌷 ☀ 🍁 ❄
TIRES USED	⊕	RACE START	🕐
		RACE FINISH	
ENGINE SIZE	⚙	FINISHING POSITION	🏁

TYRE PRESSURE		START POSITION
FRONT	REAR	
		LAPS COMPLETED
		1ST ROUND AT

FASTEST TIME	FASTEST LAP

FURTHER OBSERVATIONS

RACE EVENT		DATE
LOCATION		
KART NUMBER		/ /

RACE NUMBER IN ROW		CURRENT STANDING	
WEATHER CONDITION	☀ ☁ ❄ ⛈ 〰	TIME OF YEAR	🌷 ☀ 🍃 ❄
TIRES USED	⊚	RACE START	🕐
		RACE FINISH	
ENGINE SIZE	🔧	FINISHING POSITION	🏁

TYRE PRESSURE		START POSITION
FRONT	REAR	
		LAPS COMPLETED
		1ST ROUND AT

FASTEST TIME	FASTEST LAP

FURTHER OBSERVATIONS

RACE EVENT		DATE
LOCATION		
KART NUMBER		/ /

RACE NUMBER IN ROW		CURRENT STANDING	
WEATHER CONDITION	☀ ☁ ❄ ⚡ 🌬	TIME OF YEAR	🌷 ☀ 🍂 ❄
TIRES USED	⚙	RACE START	🕐
		RACE FINISH	
ENGINE SIZE	🔧	FINISHING POSITION	🏁

TYRE PRESSURE		START POSITION
FRONT	REAR	
		LAPS COMPLETED
		1ST ROUND AT

FASTEST TIME	FASTEST LAP

FURTHER OBSERVATIONS

RACE EVENT		DATE
LOCATION		
KART NUMBER		/ /

RACE NUMBER IN ROW		CURRENT STANDING	
WEATHER CONDITION	☀ ☁ ❄ ⛈ 🌬	TIME OF YEAR	🌷 ☀ 🍂 ❄
TIRES USED	◉	RACE START	⏱
		RACE FINISH	
ENGINE SIZE	🔧	FINISHING POSITION	🏁

TYRE PRESSURE		START POSITION
FRONT	REAR	
		LAPS COMPLETED
		1ST ROUND AT

FASTEST TIME	FASTEST LAP

FURTHER OBSERVATIONS

RACE EVENT		DATE
LOCATION		
KART NUMBER		/ /

RACE NUMBER IN ROW		CURRENT STANDING	
WEATHER CONDITION	☀ ☁ ❄ ⚡ ⇀	TIME OF YEAR	🌷 ☀ 🍁 ❄
TIRES USED	⊚	RACE START	🕐
		RACE FINISH	
ENGINE SIZE	🔧	FINISHING POSITION	🏁

TYRE PRESSURE		START POSITION
FRONT	REAR	
		LAPS COMPLETED
		1ST ROUND AT

FASTEST TIME	FASTEST LAP

FURTHER OBSERVATIONS

RACE EVENT		DATE
LOCATION		
KART NUMBER		/ /

RACE NUMBER IN ROW		CURRENT STANDING	
WEATHER CONDITION	☀ ☁ ❄ ⚡ 🌬	TIME OF YEAR	🌷 ☀ 🍃 ❄
TIRES USED	◉	RACE START	🕐
		RACE FINISH	
ENGINE SIZE	🔧	FINISHING POSITION	🏁

TYRE PRESSURE		START POSITION
FRONT	REAR	
		LAPS COMPLETED
		1ST ROUND AT

FASTEST TIME	FASTEST LAP

FURTHER OBSERVATIONS

RACE EVENT		DATE
LOCATION		
KART NUMBER		/ /

RACE NUMBER IN ROW		CURRENT STANDING	
WEATHER CONDITION	☀ ☁ ❄ ⛈ 🌬	TIME OF YEAR	🌷 ☀ 🍂 ❄
TIRES USED	⊕	RACE START	🕐
		RACE FINISH	
ENGINE SIZE	⚙	FINISHING POSITION	🏁

TYRE PRESSURE		START POSITION
FRONT	REAR	
		LAPS COMPLETED
		1ST ROUND AT

FASTEST TIME	FASTEST LAP

FURTHER OBSERVATIONS

RACE EVENT		DATE
LOCATION		
KART NUMBER		/ /

RACE NUMBER IN ROW		CURRENT STANDING	
WEATHER CONDITION	☀ ☁ ❄ ⛈ 〰	TIME OF YEAR	🌷 ☀ 🍂 ❄
TIRES USED	⬤	RACE START	🕐
		RACE FINISH	
ENGINE SIZE	🛠	FINISHING POSITION	🏁

TYRE PRESSURE		START POSITION
FRONT	**REAR**	
		LAPS COMPLETED
		1ST ROUND AT

FASTEST TIME	FASTEST LAP

FURTHER OBSERVATIONS

RACE EVENT		DATE
LOCATION		
KART NUMBER		/ /

RACE NUMBER IN ROW		CURRENT STANDING	
WEATHER CONDITION	☀ ☁ ❄ ⛈ 🌬	TIME OF YEAR	🌷 ☀ 🍂 ❄
TIRES USED	⊚	RACE START	🕐
		RACE FINISH	
ENGINE SIZE	⬡	FINISHING POSITION	🏁

TYRE PRESSURE		START POSITION
FRONT	REAR	
		LAPS COMPLETED
		1ST ROUND AT

FASTEST TIME	FASTEST LAP

FURTHER OBSERVATIONS

RACE EVENT		DATE
LOCATION		
KART NUMBER		/ /

RACE NUMBER IN ROW		CURRENT STANDING	
WEATHER CONDITION	☀ ☂ ❄ ⚡ 🌬	TIME OF YEAR	🌷 ☀ 🍃 ❄
TIRES USED	◉	RACE START	🕐
		RACE FINISH	
ENGINE SIZE	⚙	FINISHING POSITION	🏁

TYRE PRESSURE		START POSITION
FRONT	REAR	
		LAPS COMPLETED
		1ST ROUND AT

FASTEST TIME	FASTEST LAP

FURTHER OBSERVATIONS

RACE EVENT		DATE
LOCATION		
KART NUMBER		/ /

RACE NUMBER IN ROW		CURRENT STANDING	
WEATHER CONDITION	☀ ☁ ❄ ⛈ 🌬	TIME OF YEAR	🌷 ☀ 🍃 ❄
TIRES USED	◉	RACE START	🕐
		RACE FINISH	
ENGINE SIZE		FINISHING POSITION	🏁

TYRE PRESSURE		START POSITION
FRONT	**REAR**	
		LAPS COMPLETED
		1ST ROUND AT

FASTEST TIME	FASTEST LAP

FURTHER OBSERVATIONS

RACE EVENT		DATE
LOCATION		
KART NUMBER		/ /

RACE NUMBER IN ROW		CURRENT STANDING	
WEATHER CONDITION	☀ ☁ ❄ ⛈ 💨	TIME OF YEAR	🌷 ☀ 🍂 ❄
TIRES USED	⊕	RACE START	⊕
		RACE FINISH	
ENGINE SIZE		FINISHING POSITION	🏁

TYRE PRESSURE		START POSITION
FRONT	REAR	
		LAPS COMPLETED
		1ST ROUND AT

FASTEST TIME	FASTEST LAP

FURTHER OBSERVATIONS

RACE EVENT		DATE
LOCATION		
KART NUMBER		/ /

RACE NUMBER IN ROW		CURRENT STANDING	
WEATHER CONDITION	☀ ☁ ❄ ⛈ 💨	TIME OF YEAR	🌷 ☀ 🍁 ❄
TIRES USED	◎	RACE START	🕐
		RACE FINISH	
ENGINE SIZE	⚙	FINISHING POSITION	🏁

TYRE PRESSURE		START POSITION
FRONT	REAR	
		LAPS COMPLETED
		1ST ROUND AT

FASTEST TIME	FASTEST LAP

FURTHER OBSERVATIONS

RACE EVENT		DATE
LOCATION		
KART NUMBER		/ /

RACE NUMBER IN ROW		CURRENT STANDING	
WEATHER CONDITION	☀ ☁ ❄ ⛈ 🌬	TIME OF YEAR	🌷 ☀ 🍂 ❄
TIRES USED	⚙	RACE START	🕐
		RACE FINISH	
ENGINE SIZE		FINISHING POSITION	🏁

TYRE PRESSURE		START POSITION
FRONT	REAR	
		LAPS COMPLETED
		1ST ROUND AT

FASTEST TIME	FASTEST LAP

FURTHER OBSERVATIONS

RACE EVENT		DATE
LOCATION		
KART NUMBER		/ /

RACE NUMBER IN ROW		CURRENT STANDING	
WEATHER CONDITION	☀ ☁ ❄ ⚡ 〰	TIME OF YEAR	🌷 ☀ 🍂 ❄
TIRES USED	◉	RACE START	🕐
		RACE FINISH	
ENGINE SIZE	🔧	FINISHING POSITION	🏁

TYRE PRESSURE		START POSITION
FRONT	REAR	
		LAPS COMPLETED
		1ST ROUND AT

FASTEST TIME	FASTEST LAP

FURTHER OBSERVATIONS

RACE EVENT		DATE
LOCATION		
KART NUMBER		/ /

RACE NUMBER IN ROW		CURRENT STANDING	
WEATHER CONDITION	☀ ☁ ❄ ⛈ 〰	TIME OF YEAR	🌷 ☀ 🍁 ❄
TIRES USED	⊕	RACE START	🕐
		RACE FINISH	
ENGINE SIZE	🔧	FINISHING POSITION	🏁

TYRE PRESSURE		START POSITION
FRONT	REAR	
		LAPS COMPLETED
		1ST ROUND AT

FASTEST TIME	FASTEST LAP

FURTHER OBSERVATIONS

RACE EVENT		DATE
LOCATION		
KART NUMBER		/ /

RACE NUMBER IN ROW		CURRENT STANDING	
WEATHER CONDITION	☀ ☁ ❄ ⚡ 💨	TIME OF YEAR	🌷 ☀ 🍁 ❄
TIRES USED	⚙	RACE START	🕐
		RACE FINISH	
ENGINE SIZE	🔧	FINISHING POSITION	🏁

TYRE PRESSURE		START POSITION
FRONT	**REAR**	
		LAPS COMPLETED
		1ST ROUND AT

FASTEST TIME	FASTEST LAP

FURTHER OBSERVATIONS

RACE EVENT			DATE
LOCATION			
KART NUMBER			/ /

RACE NUMBER IN ROW		CURRENT STANDING	
WEATHER CONDITION	☀ ☁ ❄ ⛈ 💨	TIME OF YEAR	🌷 ☀ 🍂 ❄
TIRES USED	⦿	RACE START	🕐
		RACE FINISH	
ENGINE SIZE	⚙	FINISHING POSITION	🏁

TYRE PRESSURE		START POSITION
FRONT	REAR	
		LAPS COMPLETED
		1ST ROUND AT

FASTEST TIME	FASTEST LAP

FURTHER OBSERVATIONS

RACE EVENT		DATE
LOCATION		
KART NUMBER		/ /

RACE NUMBER IN ROW		CURRENT STANDING	
WEATHER CONDITION	☀ ☁ ❄ ⚡ 〜	TIME OF YEAR	🌷 ☀ 🍁 ❄
TIRES USED	⊚	RACE START	🕐
		RACE FINISH	
ENGINE SIZE	🔧	FINISHING POSITION	🏁

TYRE PRESSURE		START POSITION
FRONT	REAR	
		LAPS COMPLETED
		1ST ROUND AT

FASTEST TIME	FASTEST LAP

FURTHER OBSERVATIONS

RACE EVENT		DATE
LOCATION		
KART NUMBER		/ /

RACE NUMBER IN ROW		CURRENT STANDING	
WEATHER CONDITION	☀ ☁ ❄ ⛈ 🌬	TIME OF YEAR	🌷 ☀ 🍁 ❄
TIRES USED	◉	RACE START	🕐
		RACE FINISH	
ENGINE SIZE	🔧	FINISHING POSITION	🏁

TYRE PRESSURE		START POSITION
FRONT	REAR	
		LAPS COMPLETED
		1ST ROUND AT

FASTEST TIME	FASTEST LAP

FURTHER OBSERVATIONS

RACE EVENT		DATE
LOCATION		
KART NUMBER		/ /

RACE NUMBER IN ROW		CURRENT STANDING	
WEATHER CONDITION	☀ ☁ ❄ ⛈ 💨	TIME OF YEAR	🌷 ☀ 🍁 ❄
TIRES USED	⚙	RACE START	🕐
		RACE FINISH	
ENGINE SIZE	⚙	FINISHING POSITION	🏁

TYRE PRESSURE		START POSITION
FRONT	REAR	
		LAPS COMPLETED
		1ST ROUND AT

FASTEST TIME	FASTEST LAP

FURTHER OBSERVATIONS

Thanks For Reading!

Just a quick message to thank you so much for picking up one of our books! Our sincere hope is that this book has given you the value we always look to provide, and hope we can continue to produce quality books that will in anyway contribute to a better quality of life for our readers.

We are a small independent publisher based in London, UK and we work with talented authors from around the world, who dedicate every ounce of their effort to craft these memorable books for your reading pleasure.

The author of this title would love to hear about your experience with the book, and your review will go a long way to provide them with the insight and encouragement they need to keep creating the kind of books you want to read.

Your Opinion Makes a Real Difference.

If you want to let us know what you thought about the book, please visit the Amazon website and give us your review. We read every single review, no matter how long or short!

Thanks again and until the next time....

HAPPY READING!

Made in the USA
Middletown, DE
01 May 2023

29787737R00071